Pepper Growing

Learn How To Grow 5 Popular Types Of Hot Peppers

Disclamer: All photos used in this book, including the cover photo were made available under a Attribution-NonCommercial-ShareAlike 2.0 Generic and sourced from Flickr

Table of content

Introduction 4
Chapter 1 - Types and Varieties of Hot Peppers 5
1. Cherry pepper: 5
2. Anaheim pepper: 6
3. Jalapeno pepper: 7
4. Serrano pepper: 8
5. Cayenne pepper: 8
6. Tabasco pepper: 9
7. Thai pepper: 10
8. Ghost pepper: 11
9. Habanero chili pepper: 11
Chapter 2 - How to Grow Cayenne, Jalapeno and Anaheim at home? 13
How to grow Cayenne pepper at home: 13
How to grow jalapeno at home: 15
How to grow Anaheim pepper at home: 16
Chapter 3 - How to grow Cherry Pepper and Serrano Pepper at home? .. 19
How to grow cherry pepper at home: 19
How to grow Serrano pepper at home: 21
Chapter 4 - Tips to Grow Your Plants from Pests and Insects 23

Chapter 5 – Understand Planting Conditions to Grow Hot Pepper 28

Conclusion 32

Introduction

Hot peppers are extremely healthy vegetables, which are not difficult to grow. There efficaciousness lies within the fact that they are a rich source of Vitamins and other nutrients. Therefore, it is essential to provide a guide about how to grow hot peppers. In order to provide a brief elaboration regarding the fact, this book is written with all of the important pieces of information.

To begin, the book incorporates the types and various classifications of the hot pepper. Furthermore, the method to grow Jalapeno, Cayenne and Anaheim are included. In addition to this, the methods to cultivate cherry peppers as well as Serrano pepper are also discussed in here. Moreover, the book also incorporates the tips to keep pests and insects away from your plants. Finally, the understanding of overall planting conditions to grow hot peppers is also elaborated.

Therefore, this book serves as an astounding guide about growing hot peppers at home. This book is written in such a manner that it will facilitate all kinds of readers. Not only the professional gardeners, but also, the beginners will understand the tips and procedure for growing hot peppers. Thus, this book teaches the methods to grow five major kinds of hot pepper.

Chapter 1 – Types and Varieties of Hot Peppers

Despite their spicy taste and hot nature, hot peppers are still used by a number of people. These peppers come in a huge variety. Their properties like taste, color and shape varies differently. Some of them are present in tropical regions, while others are usually cultivated in comparatively dry parts of the world. Furthermore, there taste is high and their color is tempting. This chapter intends to provide a detailed analysis of the different kinds of hot peppers. Some of these peppers are as follows:

1. *Cherry pepper:*

Cherry peppers possess following properties:

i. These peppers are also known as pimento peppers.

ii. Cherry peppers are similar to a heart shape.

iii. They are around 4 inches wide and 4 inches long.

iv. These peppers are not very spicy. On a Scoville heat index, they enjoy 500 rating.

v. Mostly found as red stuffing inside the olives.

2. *Anaheim pepper:*

Anaheim peppers possess the following properties:

i. Another pepper which is not highly spicy is the Anaheim pepper.

ii. This pepper is generally reddish maroon in color. They are long and thin kind of peppers.

iii. Anaheim peppers generally possess 1000 to 5000 scoring on the Scoville heat index.

iv. Therefore, the pepper with the highest score is extremely spicy.

3. *Jalapeno pepper:*

Jalapeno peppers possess the following properties:

i. The jalapeño pepper is one of the most important and widely used forms of peppers used in the United States.

ii. Numerous individuals like it since it is hot yet not overpowering.

iii. These peppers are generally red or green with a length of 2- 3.

iv. Their Scoville heat record is around 5,000. Moreover, they can go anywhere in the range of 2,000 to 8,000.

v. At the point when utilized sparingly, they include only the perfect measure of hot flavor to most Mexican dishes.

vi. Numerous individuals additionally profound broil jalapeños loaded down with cheddar for a wonderful starter.

4. *Serrano pepper:*

Serrano peppers possess following properties:

i. The Serrano pepper looks like a jalapeno pepper. However, this pepper is much spicier.

ii. On the Scoville heat record, the Serrano pepper can be somewhere around 10,000 and 25,000. This pepper is generally little in size and green in shading.

iii. As per a general saying, if the pepper is smaller in size, they will be spicier.

5. *Cayenne pepper:*

Cayenne peppers possess the following properties:

i. This is another kind of hot pepper. Because of its spicy taste, it is used by a lot of people in food items.

ii. The cayenne pepper is red in color.

iii. It is large and utilized in powdered structure.

iv. Furthermore, this pepper has been utilized as a part of common prescriptions for a long time because of reported recuperating traits.

6. *Tabasco pepper:*

Tabasco peppers possess the following properties:

i. The Tabasco pepper is utilized to make Tabasco sauce.

ii. In the event that you have ever tasted how hot Tabasco sauce is, you will not be astounded to discover that the Tabasco pepper has a Scoville heat list of somewhere around 30,000 and 60,000.

iii. The real pepper is under 2 crawls in length and can be green, red, yellow or orange in shading.

7. *Thai pepper:*

Thai peppers possess the following properties:

i. The Thai pepper is grown in Thailand along with some of the other neighboring countries.

ii. It is one of the spiciest peppers of its family. Its score on a Scoville index differs from 50,000 to 100,000. Interestingly, these peppers enhance thee taste in such a manner that the person eating the food will keep on drooling over the food.

iii. The Thai pepper is one of the littlest peppers, measuring in at not exactly an inch.

iv. It is utilized as a part of the numerous fiery Thai dishes at eateries in the U.S.

inch of soil is dry to the touch. Satisfactory and unfaltering watering system is vital for most extreme natural product generation and organic product size.

7. Treat pepper plants, taking after producer's proposals, or utilize half-quality all the more frequently for a consistent supply of supplements. A compost mix with higher phosphorous than nitrogen helps peppers deliver more natural product. Overwintering pruned peppers can be treated with a higher nitrogen equation to empower rich development, decreasing nitrogen again in the spring.

How to grow jalapeno at home:
The procedure to grow jalapeno pepper at home is as follows:

1. Sow seeds around two months from the time you need to transplant them into your greenhouse. Put two seeds in little pots loaded with the blend of soil. Plant seeds about quarter crawl profound. Water altogether.

2. Put the pots in a sunny window. Keep up the temperature at 80 degrees Fahrenheit, since jalapenos require a dirt temperature of 80 degrees Fahrenheit to sprout well.

3. Check the dirt temperature with a thermometer. Keep the plant watered; however not saturated. Pivot the pot a fourth of a turn every four days if the light source is a window. On the off chance that both seeds sprout, evacuate the weakest one.

4. Take care of your plant by providing the suitable conditions for it. Moreover, regularly provide water as well as the required sunlight to ensure a proper growth of your plant. Transplant it after all risk of ice is past.

How to grow Anaheim pepper at home:
If you intend to grow Anaheim pepper at home, then you must follow the steps given below:

1. Develop Anaheim pepper in a sunny zone of the greenery enclosure that has all around depleted soil. Besides, the pH of the soil must exist in 5 and 7. You can do various tests in order to measure the pH of the soil you are working on. In order to regulate the pH, you can add various chemicals in the soil accordingly. As indicated by the test outcomes, revise the dirt with limestone to raise the pH, or fuse sulfur to lower it. Moreover, addition of fertilizers can also help in the maintenance of the dampness of your soil. Transplant the seedlings when the dirt temperature surpasses fifty degrees Fahrenheit.

2. Mulch the dirt with dark plastic before transplanting the seedlings in the event that you live in a cooler region or on the off chance that you need to begin your plants early. Notwithstanding warming the dirt, the plastic additionally advances soil-dampness maintenance and keeps weeds under control. Grow the plants after creating small holes.

3. Care must be taken and one must sow the Anaheim seed with appropriate space. All of the seeds must be spaced 2 feet apart in lines. Moreover, these lines must be separated from each other by a distance of 3 feet. In addition, the area in between the beds must be 14 inches for proper growth with the provision of wide area.

4. Water Anaheim Chili properly in the entire developing season. Moreover, keep the dirt consistently damp. If the soil is dry then it can hinder the growth of your plant. Above all, try not to spray the soil which is not to be used afterwards.

5. Presently, include some manure in the planting bed. Disseminate 2 tablespoons of manure in a trench which is dug around all of the plants. The trench must be 4 inches farther from the stem of the plant and abstain from getting manure on the plant. Addition of the manure at nearer places can burn the plant. Then again, burrow a 1-inch-profound long trench on either side of a column and the soil mixture in them. Afterwards, fulfill the trench, water them and clean them properly.

6. Wash your hands with a cleanser and water before taking care of Anaheim pepper. Moreover, one must not smoke near the plants. Tobacco can trigger plants to build up the Tobacco Mosaic Virus, which stains the foods grown from the ground the leaves to yellow and build up a mosaic example. Hence, if you want to have healthy yields, use gloves as well.

Chapter 3 – How to grow Cherry Pepper and Serrano Pepper at home?

Cherry peppers as well as Serrano peppers are two other major types of hot pepper. It is extremely simple to grow them at the house. Moreover, the cherry peppers as well as the Serrano peppers possess high nutritional values. These peppers are not only used to control cholesterol level, but also, they are used to eradicate the chances of arthritis.

How to grow cherry pepper at home:
The method to grow cherry pepper at home is given below:

1. One must develop pepper plants in proper sunlight. Once the temperature reaches fifty degrees Fahrenheit in the evening, the right time for plantation has come.

2. Pour fertilizer into the dirt before planting. Dig holes and add manures. This will improve the nature of the plant. Moreover, they will also help in the growth. Add the soil to fulfill these holes. Water them appropriately.

3. Include natural fertilizers to improve the growth of your plant. These plants will need mulch as well. Once you have included the mulch, you are good to go.

4. Water the cherry peppers instantly after they are planted. The amount of water must be such that it wets the soil but the water content does not exceed the desired level. However, if such a situation occurs that the plants become dry, then add the sufficient but not extra amount of water.

5. Once the plant is loaded with one or two small fruits, then you can gather them. In order to gather these, use scissors to cut the peppers. Try not to pluck them with your hands as they are spicy and can cause burn in the area.

How to grow Serrano pepper at home:
The method to use Serrano pepper at home, one must follow the steps given below:

1. To begin, sow the seeds of in a pot with a homemade soil mixture. Seed develops best when soil temperature is 70F or higher. However, if the temperature is below fifty, then various problems can take place in the process of germination.

2. Moreover, one must not place these plants in the light deficient areas. If these plants do not get proper sunlight, they fail to grow.

3. Do not place your plants outside in ice cold weather. If the plants are hampered because of the snow, then it becomes extremely difficult to save them and grow other plants.

4. Move the plants outside once the soil is warm and pleasant. If the soil is not appropriate, then do not take the plants outside.

5. Use dark plastic or column spreads to speed soil warming and early development. Use various homemade manures to warm up the soil. This will help in the growth of the plant.

6. If you do not desire to use dark plastic, then you must mulch the plants after they are settled. This will maintain the dampness of your soil. Moreover, they will also help in controlling the weeds.

7. Peppers are sensitive when the temperature reaches extreme conditions. They face problems in both extremely hot as well as in the extreme cold weathers. Therefore, you must choose mild temperature with enough sunlight.

8. A large amount of nitrogen manure may advance the rich vegetative development. Moreover, these peppers have depicted positive response to phosphorus manure as well. However, with the addition of a chemical, the organic component of your fruit will be decreased.

9. Furthermore, try to maintain even levels of calcium and other nutrients in the soil as well.

Chapter 4 – Tips to Grow Your Plants from Pests and Insects

Growing vegetables in your own garden provides you great opportunities and variety of food. However, if proper care is not taken, then these vegetable can be attacked by numerous pests and insects. In this way, bug control is very essential to avoid such issues. On the negative side, pesticides contain large amounts of perilous poisons that may leave its residues on the foods grown from the ground. Astoundingly, natural pesticides which are home-made are safer and efficacious. In addition, they can be produced using each one of those things which are not expansive.

Utilization of the following homemade recipes can be used to grow plants and keep pests away:

1. **Garlic Sprays:**

   The strong fragrance of garlic keeps numerous insects away from the vegetables. For this common pesticide, blend 10 to 12 garlic cloves with 1 quart of water and mix them together. Now allow the mixture to settle for 24 hours. Afterwards, strain it through cheesecloth covering the opening of a glass container and incorporate 1 cup of cooking oil. This concentrated mixture works efficiently for a number of days. In order to increase the efficiency, put one tablespoon of cayenne pepper in a jar and place it in the mixture you have created. Now let it stay for an extra 24 hours before straining the liquid. Strain the liquid and you are now good to use the spray.

2. Red Chili Pepper:

This pepper is widely known for its ability to add taste in pizza and to incorporate flavors in the food items. In a similar manner, red pepper powder can be used to make a locally developed pesticide that is efficient enough to keep pests and insects away. In order to make the mixture, blend 1 tablespoon of red pepper powder, 6 drops of washing powder and 1 gallon of water and mix all of them together. Sprinkle the pepper spray on the vegetables as per the requirement. In order to get better outcomes, reapply the spray. This will keep the pests away.

3. Vinegar:

It works especially well for weeds in the garden. The essential issue with vinegar is that it can hurt numerous varieties of plants. In this way, it is recommended to use a pad to brush the vinegar particularly onto the leaves of the weeds one is endeavoring to execute. This keeps the vinegar from getting onto distinctive plants and ensures that the entire leaf surface is secured with the vinegar.

4. Cleanser and Alcohol Sprays:

To start, blend a teaspoon of fluid cleanser in some rubbing liquor in one quart of water. Once you have thoroughly mixed them, you can apply them on the plants. However, before the application, test the mixture on two or three leaves to guarantee no harm is done to the plants. Sprinkle the solution on the top and base of leaves to protect them. Moreover, you can also apply this mixture using a pad or a brush. Once you have applied the mixture, and then wait for some time. After a few minutes, wash the leaves swiftly with cold water.

5. Baby Shampoo Sprays:

A baby shampoo is very effective yet harmless cleanser. Moreover, it does not contain any chemicals. On the contrary, if there are some chemicals present in the shampoo, then their content ratio is extremely low. Therefore, it can be used to keep away numerous insects. This spray can protect indoor as well as the outdoor plants, including aphids, scales and insect vermin.

6. Lime Sulfur:

Lime sulfur is an old but still used cure for pests. It is used by both professional and simple gardeners. This blend is used to kill most sorts of pests. In addition, it is also used to eradicate eggs of insects and other insects. Lime sulfur also has fungicidal impact and can be used on normal and ornamentals trees. On the brighter side, care must be taken since lime sulfur associated with plants near the house will recolor the paint. Apply as per the requirement.

7. Tobacco Water:

Strangely, tobacco and cigarette butts are helpful for eradicating worms. They can be used to kill various species of aphids and termites, In order to create tobacco water, blend tobacco along with water to create a blend that creates a brownish mixture. After the mixture is settled, put it on the soil. However, keep this mixture away from the children as it can be extremely dangerous if drunk.

8. Oil Sprays:

Firstly, take 1 tablespoon of washing agent and include 1 cup of cooking oil from a fresh oil bottle. This concentrated liquid must be mixed with water before use with an extent of 4 teaspoons of oil mix to 1 half quart of water until the mixture is completely ready. At that moment, place the oil mixture in a glass container in a calm, dry and cool area. Apply little parts of this spray on the affected areas. This will keep the mites and midges away from your pepper.

Some of the advantages of using these natural pesticides are as follow:

i. Economical:

Making your own pesticides is extremely beneficial since it costs less and provides encouraging results. By far most of the responses for these pesticides are overwhelming. They are extremely economical and beneficial.

ii. Secure:

These mixtures include those ingredients which are secure. Therefore, they are used by many farmers as well as ordinary gardeners.

iii. Non-Toxin:

> Most of the homemade pesticides do not use substances that contain harmful ingredients. They possess nontoxic ingredients and efficacious results. Therefore, they are extremely beneficial.

Therefore, the use of homemade pesticides to improve the growth of your plants is extremely beneficial. They will provide you an opportunity to enhance the quality of your work by simply using those substances, which are easily available at your home. Moreover, these pesticides do not possess any harmful ingredient that might cause problems to the growth of your plants. The ingredients utilized are easily available in the grocery stores and used in various houses as common items. Therefore, one must use these homemade pesticides to get maximum advantage.

Chapter 5 – Understand Planting Conditions to Grow Hot Pepper

Plant the peppers on such areas which receive adequate sunlight. To begin, choose a soil that contains high minerals and is not attacked by any of the pests or insects. Moreover, the soil must not be saline. Afterwards, dig holes to plant the seeds; however, maintain appropriate spacing between the holes. As a result, the plants will get enough space for their growth. Moreover, manures and fertilizers must be added in order to improve the condition of the soil. In addition, maintain a thorough record of the plantation date. In this way, you will succeed in eradicating the growth issues. Moreover, you will be able to maintain and follow a complete timeline of the plant growth. Some of the important things and tips which must be understood before growing the peppers are included in this chapter. Following are the conditions used to grow hot pepper:

Cultivate using plant or seeds:

Usually the gardeners with efficient skills and abilities try to cultivate these hot peppers. However, a large portion of us must begin planting our own particular plants 8-10 weeks before transplanting, which ought to be done 2-3 weeks after the normal last ice.

Most pepper seeds sprout grow at a temperature of 70 degrees F.; however, germination can be hampered if the temperature is not appropriate. Hot peppers can be extremely tricky at time. Moreover, they might demand warm soil for their growth. To speed up the procedure, put the seeds between sodden sheets of paper towel, place them in zippered plastic packs, and put the sack in a warm place. When the pepper seeds sprout, deliberately plant them in individual holders, for example, pea pots. At the point when the main leaves emerge, move the plants to a sunny southern window until you can transplant them into the garden. Try not to set out your pepper transplants until night temperatures reach around 55 degrees F.

How to cultivate:

Cultivation of hot pepper can be challenging at times; however, it is not difficult if handled properly. In order to get better results, two tips must be followed while cultivating the hot peppers:

1. **Water with some restraint:**

   Peppers are parched plants. They require a moderate supply of water from the minute they grow until the end of the season. In any case, peppers won't endure a soaked soil that waterlogs their roots. The dirt must deplete well, yet hold enough dampness to keep the plants underway. To keep up a legitimate equalization, before transplanting, work some natural matter in the dirt to upgrade dampness maintenance. Use mulch to keep unreasonable vanishing from the dirt amid the dry summer months.

2. **Do not over-treat:**

   This tends to make the pepper plants create rich foliage to the detriment of natural product generation. Put a normal ratio of fertilizer on plants. You can likewise side-dress the plants with a light sprinkling when blooming begins, just to give them a help if necessary.

Tips to improve growth:

To enhance general pepper generation, consider utilizing the accompanying systems.

1. **Plastic Mulch:**

   To get an ambitious start with your peppers, cover the readied bed with dim hued polyethylene mulch a week prior to transplanting. This will warm the dirt underneath and give a superior developing condition to youthful pepper plants. The mulch will likewise help the dirt hold dampness all through the season as the plants develop.

2. **Sidekick Plantation:**

   Another technique to improve the growth is to plant other vegetables. Some of the sidekick plants are tomatoes, parsley, basil, and carrots. Try not to plant peppers close to fennel.

Tips to harvest:

The harvest time is very important in case of a hot pepper growth. As the pepper differs in its taste at different levels, it is essential to harvest them at the point when they have achieved maximum flavor. Despite these peppers can be used without any harm at all stages, yet it is recommended to use the, after they are fully ripped. In order to harvest the hot peppers properly, some tips must be followed. The tips that might prove beneficial while harvesting the peppers:

1. Similar to summer squashes and cucumbers, peppers can be generally gathered at any stage. The usually used pepper, for instance, is collected green. Despite the fact that most fruits will turn red, orange, or yellow.

Peppers can be collected at any phase of development; however they develop their complete taste when they are completely ripened. Therefore, to get better results, one must wait longer

2. Successive reaping builds yields. If you pluck un-ripped fruits then the plants might suffer in the future as well.

3. Permitting natural products to completely age upgrades flavor as well as the yield. Additionally, you will need to hold up until late in the season before collecting table-prepared peppers.

4. In order to eradicate the chances of less fruit production, one must plant two or three plants at a time. Permit one plant of every plant to completely age to develop, and harvest the other all through the season. Likewise, when you are picking peppers, abstain from pulling on the organic product, which may sever a branch or even evacuate the whole plant. Utilize a sharp blade or garden shears to cut the intense stem.

Conclusion

Plantation of hot peppers is a common activity in many tropical areas, used in various food items to add spicy touch to the dish. This book incorporates various pieces of information starting from the elaboration of various unique and spicy hot peppers to the procedure used to grow these. Interestingly, there are a large number of hot peppers; however, this book focuses on five of the major kinds of these peppers; namely, Cayenne pepper, Jalapeno pepper, Anaheim pepper, Cherry pepper as well as Serrano pepper.

In addition, in this book, the tips are included which will help the gardener in keeping harmful insects and pests away. The book does not only contain these tips, but the quintessential environment to grow these plants included as well. These conditions must be fulfilled in order to eradicate any damage to the plant. If these conditions are not met, then the plants will not grow properly. They might fail to provide any fruit. Moreover, the growth might also be hindered.

Hence, this book incorporates the complete detail about the ideal procedure to grow hot peppers on your own. These grown peppers will be healthy, nutritious and inexpensive.